A Dog's Five Essential Needs

THE FIVE THINGS YOUR DOG REQUIRES TO HAVE A HEALTHY AND HAPPY LIFE

Saro Boghozian, Certified Expert Family Dog Trainer

ISBN: 1505573076
ISBN 13: 9781505573077

I'd like to dedicate this book to my dad. He sacrificed his life and helped me to be where I am today and taught me to never give up and go further in life.

CONTENTS

ABOUT THIS BOOK

I love educating dog owners, and I feel education is very important. One of my goals is educating dog owners about their pets. The emphasis of this book is on building a healthier relationship with your dog rather than on improving dog ownership. Unfortunately, many dog owners are not able to build a real and healthy relationship with their dogs. While many dog owners are physically there with their dogs, they are emotionally absent. I hope that by reading this book you will have better ideas for preventing unstable behaviors in your dog and for developing healthier strategies for improving your relationship with your dog.

This book is written for people who are thinking of getting a dog and for those who already have one. It is designed to help you create a healthier, more balanced relationship while preventing issues, thereby allowing your dog to live a better life.

In this book, I will introduce you to proven practices that, if followed, will lead to success. You will be able to see changes in yourself—and in your dog's life—while learning what you need to know about dogs.

These practices focus on a dog's five essential needs. I will explain what the essential dog needs are, analyzing each one in detail so you have a solid understanding of each concept.

This information will guide you and give you some ideas about how to prepare before you get a dog or make changes if you already have one, plus how to maintain your dog's health physically, mentally, and emotionally for years to come.

INTRODUCTION

There are several reasons I wanted to write this book. One of them was to give dog owners ideas about how to deal with their dog.

The other reason was that I wanted to teach people what I have figured out in many years of my practice as a dog trainer. Before becoming a trainer, I was a typical dog owner and I used to make many mistakes when it came to my dog. For instance, I thought dogs could eat everything, not knowing that they should not eat certain things such as grapes and raisins, which may actually kill them. Or when dogs pant, it is not because they are happy; it is because they are either hot or stressed. This lack of knowledge may have caused my dog and me several headaches. I want to help dog owners avoid making the kinds of mistakes I made.

The goal of training dogs and educating dog owners for me has always been to help them create a "balanced" dog. Many people ask me, "What is a balanced dog?" A balanced dog is a dog that can tolerate new situations and conditions easily. The new situation could be, for example, the gathering of family members, and the dog should be able to tolerate them without getting nervous or stressed. A new condition could be something like entering a building with new floors that the dog has never stepped on, or when the dog sees and feels rain or snow for the first time.

A balanced dog is able to obey and follow humans. This not only makes the dog's life easier, it also makes it tolerable to live with them. Dogs should be attentive to humans when we ask them to sit or come. We need them to respond to us even when we tell them, "No, don't do that," or "Yes, that was right, good boy." Dogs are capable of communicating with us as long as we try to communicate with them.

When a dog is able to tolerate new situations and conditions while obeying humans, it is able to live a healthier and more relaxed life and can therefore focus on being a good, balanced dog.

The reality is that dogs are pets and should be considered pets. They are not humans with four paws or babies with furry bodies. They are domesticated animals that have been invited to live with humans. They are animals, but they are man-made. Did you know that some of the breeds you see today didn't exist even fifty years ago?

It is important to remember that dogs are domesticated animals. They are not wild animals or human babies. Dog owners confuse dogs by treating them like humans or humanizing them. They forget how to behave like dogs, and they learn and practice behaviors that humans feel are the norm. When a dog behaves like a human, humans celebrate it. But making a dog act and behave like a human is unfair. How would you feel if dogs treated humans like dogs?

We should allow dogs to be dogs and ask dogs to respect and treat us like humans.

This is why dog owners need to learn about dogs and what makes them good dogs.

Chapter 1

UNDERSTANDING DOGS

We are fortunate to have dogs in our lives. We should be thankful we can have them live with us, especially in this day and age, when humans are largely disconnected from nature. Instead of connecting with nature, we focus on artificial ways of satisfying the need to spend time outdoors.

Dogs can remind us of this important part of our lives, which is so often sacrificed for a metropolitan lifestyle. They can teach us to slow down, take it easy, and smell the roses—literally. Many people have forgotten how to do this and need to learn to be patient, to relax, and to be one with nature.

Even as we try to take a more natural approach to what we eat and the way we live, we forget that dogs are naturally organic and can help us achieve a balanced state of mind and the lifestyle we seek. The signs are right by our feet. We should take clues from our dogs, but we don't. We live in a fast-paced environment that is the opposite of a dog's biological system. Dogs live shorter lives than humans; they are not consumed with the future. All they think about is now; therefore, they are not living in a fast-evolving society. They live based on instincts, which tell them to live in a certain slow, simple way, the way nature intended. Nature takes time to evolve and regenerate. Dogs and animals follow nature's path. They take their time. They do not rush to work, for instance. They have all day to spend on their owner's couch. Dog owners rush to work or other places, and in the dog's mind, humans are unbalanced because they are not relaxed.

Dogs remind us of the benefits of living at a slow pace, of living in the moment, but we pay no attention to them and the message they are sending us. Dogs are constantly communicating to us, telling us to slow down. A few of my clients have gone through tough times in their lives, and the only way they could cope was to have a dog.

Dogs become listeners to the negativity the owner expresses, acting as sponges, absorbing all that negativity. This happens even when times aren't tough. The dog sees, hears, feels, smells, and senses all the negativity a family shares with it unwittingly, and the dog cannot say anything. So dogs express their stress and frustration in neurotic forms of behavior.

We make them suffer because of our ignorance. We care more about possessions than about giving the right care to our best friends, who care so much about us. We forget that our dogs have emotions and feelings just like us. They can also be happy, mad, and sad. They can become emotionally unbalanced, angry, and careless if we don't care for their mental state and focus on ways to make them happy or keep them busy. Sometimes ignoring their feelings can lead to complicated behaviors, causing them to become so badly behaved that they have to be put down. Many dogs are being put down because they are stressed and confused when their humans have ignored what they have been trying to communicate.

Dogs come in many breeds, colors, shapes, and sizes. These varieties and options have led to a range of issues and complications.

Because of the line of business I am in, I mostly have to deal with the ugly situations that dog owners create. I have seen the dark side of this story. I have seen dogs begging to be rescued from the confinements in which they have been trapped with their humans.

Dog owners purchase all kinds of tools and gadgets to improve their dogs' bad behaviors, yet the behaviors never change or sometimes get worse. People buy the most expensive leash and collar set they can find, but they don't walk their dog on a leash properly because their dogs do not know how to walk on leash. Some dogs want to kill other dogs, animals, and people. Other dogs have developed sensitivity to particular sounds or objects. They jump on people or bite kids and adults. These are all unusual behaviors that dog owners do not expect from their dogs, but most dogs exhibit these behaviors. In most cases, dog owners have no idea that their dogs exhibit unusual behaviors until one day dog owners get surprised. They think if a dog is behaving a certain way, such as jumping on people or being neurotic or fearful, then it must be normal. They don't realize that most of these so-called normal behaviors are the reasons most major bad behaviors develop. I've seen all of these behaviors—dogs that are nervous, can't relax, can't stay calm for long periods of time, get excited quickly, get upset or reactive to certain things, bark at everything, shake or shiver, bite people, lick themselves obsessively, etc.

Before we focus on the good side of dogs, we need to know what happens when we do not do the right things and do not take the right steps.

The Causes of Bad Behavior
There are many reasons why dogs develop undesirable behaviors. Bad breeding, overbreeding, improper socialization, improper environments and people to grow with, lack of needs being met, lack of dog owners' knowledge, lack of training, and not

being raised properly have all caused dogs to be unbalanced and unpredictable.

Dog owners wonder why their dogs behave badly, but the reality is that dog owners can often be the main contributors to creating this dark side. I believe dog owners are the problem—and therefore the solution—because we should be responsible for our actions. Dog owners are the ones who choose to get dogs, and they must be fully responsible for their dogs.

The beauty of dogs is that they are task oriented. Dogs are followers and want to do what you want them to do. The fact is, if you articulate the desire for a dog to protect you, it will do the best it can to protect you; if you ask the dog to be a listener to your daily problems, it will do the best job it can listening to your problems. They will sacrifice themselves unknowingly yet willingly for their owners in whatever ways it takes. They can also give back a hundred times more than you give to them.

One other trait of dogs is that they want to live balanced lives naturally. They are born that way—balanced, normal, and happy. They want to enjoy life and enjoy a partnership with their humans and surroundings. They want to satisfy their humans, to please them so the humans can provide just a little more for them. They don't ask for much but in return, they often receive mental and emotional baggage from their humans. This causes them to go into overload mode and blow up. This is when the dog starts showing unusual behaviors, which results in his human calling him a badly behaved dog.

Dogs come in many breeds, colors, shapes, and sizes. These varieties and options have led to a range of issues and complications when it comes to selecting dogs as pets. Choosing a dog based on looks, color, and size can be a misstep when other important options such as compatibility, capability, and overall ability to own a dog have been ignored. Sometimes the selection is also an emotional decision. The dog is selected because the human feels sorry for the dog, regardless of whether the human is compatible with the dog or is able to provide for the dog emotionally and physically. In some cases, the dog becomes an accessory for entertainment for the kids or a certain family member.

Selecting a dog based on looks or on an emotionally driven decision often creates an unfortunate situation for the dog, which leads to mental, physical, and emotional neglect. I am not talking about not providing food or shelter for the dog; I am talking about neglecting dogs on a psychological level, which is one of the severest forms of neglect. Even with the best care, the latest fashions, the best beds, and the best material life, dogs are not happy and are overstressed. Oftentimes it is the dog owner who is the instigator of a domino effect in the dog's life.

Let me explain this issue by giving you an example. I had been called to a couple's home for a consultation about their dog's behavioral issues. After meeting the couple, I met the dog. He looked very nervous to me. I knew right then and there what the problem was—actually, I knew the problem and the solution even before I got the call from them.

I began by asking them the usual question: What problem do you have with your dog? One of them started telling me their dog was reactive to certain sounds and objects, either in the house or at the park, and because of that the dog started to bark and bite everyone for no reason. The dog was unpredictable.

Next I asked them to describe to me a regular daily routine of their dog. One of them explained that when they got up in the morning, one of them would take the dog out, depending on who had gotten up the day before. Then they fed the dog breakfast. If the wife was working from home that day, the husband would take off for work, and the wife would keep the dog home, playing with or walking the dog a couple of times a day, if possible, until the husband came home and took the dog out for a good, long walk—if the husband was not tired.

All of a sudden, the discussion took on a life of its own—the wife told the husband that he never wakes up in the morning to walk the dog, which led to them arguing about the fact that she never lets him choose things that are needed for the home, he never helps with the groceries, she never does any of the office work, and he never walks the dog. Basically, for the hour I sat with them, I ended up listening to a couple argue about their lives together; the dog was mentioned maybe once.

I looked at their dog, and the dog looked back at me and silently begged, "Please help me." If I lived with this couple, I would have snapped at anything, too. I would have gone mental. So I asked them to take the dog for a walk. During the walk I explained what the problems were. The dog's bad behavior was his way of telling them, "Mom, Dad, please get along and be my caretakers. I don't want to be a burden. I need you to be calm and relaxed."

The couple never imagined that they were the reason the dog was misbehaving. They thought there was something wrong with their dog, but in reality there was something wrong with their relationship. The dog was involuntarily involved in their messy relationship.

In this and many other cases, dogs go through a variety of scenarios in which the owners cause the issues, physically or mentally. Dogs, in my opinion, are natural barometers, gauges for a family's balance. If you have a dog that is unbalanced, it is because the dog sees you and your family as somehow unbalanced. I understand—nobody's perfect. But a dog cannot help feeding off the family dynamics, and he will become a part of them, no matter what the dynamics are. The dynamics can be positive or negative, and the dog will respond to those accordingly. Dogs want to be a part of whatever is happening, positive or negative. It is in their nature to join in.

In general, the motives, the causes, the levels of mental harm, and the issues are different from one case to another, but the underlying reasons are all the same. The reality is that a dog can get stressed from living with an unbalanced human. Unfortunately, some dogs live with unbalanced humans who are busy with their lives—busy with everything else but the dog.

One of the sad facts is that dog owners choose to have busy lives and to have dogs. It is not fair for the dogs to get into an environment that is not ideal for them. Some dog owners have hectic lives and hope to stabilize their lives, to deal with their issues, by getting a dog. This often backfires. Instead creating a suitable situation for the dog and the dog owners, the dog becomes one more issue for them to deal with. Using a dog to deal with issues is like sweeping the issues under the rug—they are there but not visible until the dog drags them out for all to see.

Dog owners sometimes feel as if they are doing everything they can to change the situation, and yet they don't see results. That is because their lives are prioritized over the dogs. They just want to have their dog available when they are available physically. When they come home and are in need of something to pet. They need a dog to relieve their daily stress. They want to have their dog because they love the dog. Now the unbalanced human is attached to an unbalanced dog.

Most dog behaviors that become "the issue" for dog owners are accumulations of several unaddressed issues that have led to anxiety for the dog. "The issue" stands out from the other issues because it causes the owners headaches and, probably, embarrassment. They don't realize that their dog is misbehaving because of more than just "the issue."

Most times when behaviors become "the issue," it is due to a combination of many other issues that have led to anxiety in the dog. For example, if a dog isn't introduced to the vacuum cleaner properly, he may develop anxiety toward it, experiencing a fight-or-flight reaction. If these kinds of situations happen often, with different objects, scenarios, and experiences, the dog experiences the same reaction and develops more anxiety. Meanwhile, there might be other issues and objects that build up even more anxiety within the dog.

Let's say that one day your dog is in a park, and several dogs surround him for play. But your dog translates this as being trapped or as threatening. This new situation, plus all those stressors that have piled up, become a volcano of emotions. The dog erupts and reacts in the form of attacking those dogs.

You interpret the incident as your dog being reactive to some friendly dogs—as if your dog is misbehaving—not realizing that it is not just that incident that has caused your dog to act in an extreme manner. This becomes "the issue" that bothers you now, but it is the result of several issues that you have not addressed accordingly.

Prevention is one of the key words I need to emphasize. Dog owners need to be able to prevent dogs from building bad behaviors, but instead, most people unknowingly help their dogs develop the behavior. It is far easier to prevent the behaviors from developing than to deal with the behaviors after they have developed.

I will give you an example. One day a client called and asked me if I could help her deal with her dog jumping on people. This was happening every time guests would come to her home. I agreed to take the case.

"Are there any other things you don't like about your dog?" I asked during our first meeting.

"Not really," she replied. "Just that the dog is nippy sometimes."

"Is that all?" I asked.

"Well, there are times when the dog barks at the neighbor."

"Only one neighbor or all the neighbors?"

"No, just that particular neighbor."

"Is that it?" I asked again.

"Well, the dog sometimes counter-surfs."

"OK, is there anything else?"

"No. Other than these, the dog is perfect," she responded.

I am fairly certain that, if I had continued to probe, I would have gotten a longer list of bad behaviors that, from the dog owner's point of view, seemed unimportant. But all of those behaviors are bad behaviors that should be addressed. Instead, the dog owner chose to ignore them.

To address the dog's jumping on people, I had to start by teaching the owner that she needed to address all the unwanted bad behaviors—she couldn't address only one.

The beauty of this story is that after a month of my working with the owner, not only did the dog stop jumping on the people, but the dog owner also prevented him from developing other bad behaviors. However, if the dog owner had prevented each bad behavior as it presented itself, the dog would not have developed any bad habits in the first place.

If you want to address "the issue," you need to address all of the issues.

There are other reasons that can cause dogs to become unbalanced.

Most people own a dog for companionship. The reality is that dog owners are not fulfilling their end of the bargain. Some dogs are not happy, and some dogs have developed unhealthy, strange, erratic behaviors that even surprise professionals like me.

Lifestyles have changed, and these changes are having an impact on all aspects of our society. Our lives are not as they used to be, compared to even ten years ago. Things have changed significantly.

Dogs, on the other hand, have been bred for the same reasons and purposes as they used to be, but they are not able to live the same way they used to live—on farms or in houses that have huge backyards, with live animals all over the place. Dogs used to grow up socializing and interacting with all the things around them, including kids, cats, other live animals, cars, trucks, and people.

Today, dogs are brought to houses and condos that have neighbors who don't want to deal with someone else's dog; they have to encounter cars and streets that are noisy and scary and family members who are busy with everything but them. Dogs are confused living in an environment that is so far removed from the ideal place for them to live, yet they are forced to adjust and settle in—no matter what breed they are.

Today, because of urbanization, designer breed dogs are more popular. Yet dogs are still bred the same way or in even worse ways (thanks to puppy mills) but not for the same intention. Today most dog owners get a dog based on needs like as a substitute for children; as a fashion statement; for their looks, color, or size; but not for what the dog is capable of doing. The dog is often selected based on what the family likes, what looks good for them, and what they want the dog to represent.

Consequently, all breeds of dogs become fair game to fulfill this one purpose—filling a spot that is empty in human lives. Often, this role is not suited for the dog. Working dogs become lap dogs, so they become unemployed and retire at the age of one. To some, all breeds need to have one job, to be a pet, rather than to be able to be what they are—a domesticated working animal. In a way, many dog breeds become retired working dogs as soon as they join human families.

These unemployed dogs have the tendency to become unbalanced and dangerous in our society if proper exercise, training, and socialization are not provided for them. To make things worse, dogs are not allowed to be involved in our society when they don't behave appropriately, which in turn can cause more undesirable issues with our dogs. Basically, most dogs do not have the social skills to be involved naturally in our human society.

The other term I like to emphasize is "responsibility." If you get a dog, you need to agree 100 percent that you are responsible for all of your dog's actions. You need to accept that you are the cause of your dog's behaviors and actions, and you need to commit to that responsibility.

Many dog owners, because they don't know much about dogs, tend to blame their dogs' misbehaviors on something else and only take credit for their dogs' good behavior. Good dog behavior is developed only by training and working with a dog. If a dog owner invests time and effort in helping the dog develop good behavior, then he or she should definitely take credit for it. But when a dog is misbehaving, it is because the owner has not invested enough time to teach the dog good behavior. Therefore, the dog does not know how to behave properly. That is why I blame dog owners for the dog's bad behavior.

Solutions

The greatest problem is that most families are not prepared for, or their lifestyles are not suitable for, a dog, yet they get one anyway. People make the choice with their hearts and not with their minds, which often leads to choosing the wrong breed or dog.

Having a well-behaved, balanced dog requires lots of work. The decision to have a dog for most people is easier than deciding which coffeemaker to buy. People spend more time educating themselves about and shopping for coffeemakers than they do learning about different breeds of dogs and choosing one that is suitable for them. People who want to own a dog must be willing to get educated before getting a dog. Most people do it backward—get the dog and then start the education process. Some believe that they just need to train the dog once they get it, but the reality is that dog owners need to be educated first in order to educate their dogs. That is the first step to creating balance.

You shouldn't wait to try to train your dog until after you see misbehavior; by then it is somewhat late. By starting a regular training system from the beginning, you can prevent the development of behavioral issues. Training yourself should start before you get the dog. First you need to educate and train yourselves about dogs, breeds, and what it takes to own a dog. Next, choose the right dog for your family, one that fits your lifestyle. Then start training your new dog and continue training your dog for years.

Dog owners feel they are in strange territory when they deal with their dogs. They are confused about what to do, how to approach their dogs' issues, and how to raise a well-behaved, balanced dog. When dog owners realize they do not have the knowledge they need to take care of their dogs properly, it becomes frustrating, both for the dog owners and the dogs. This leads to dog owners developing fear or anxiety around their dogs, creating even more stress and developing even more distance in the relationship.

Chief Dan George said, "If you talk to animals, they will talk with you and you will know each other. If you don't talk to them, you will not know them and what you do not know you will fear. What one fears, one destroys."

The other problem I've encountered with dog owners is the way they gather information about dogs and the way they educate themselves. There are three common issues dog owners run into when looking for information: too much information, outdated and unproven information, and not following through on solid information.

There are hundreds of ideas and opinions out there (especially on the Internet) about how to train your dog. This can confuse dog owners who just want "the answer." It's hard to choose which idea, which opinion, will work best for one specific dog owner and his or her dog. I believe an opinion has to make sense to the dog owner. It has to be accepted and believed in. Then the dog owner needs to stick to that idea and follow through with it; otherwise it will not work out, no matter what the idea is.

There are many training systems, ideas, and opinions about how to train your dog, how to deal with dog issues, how to raise a dog, and so on. Most of the systems may work for you and your dog, and the issues that you have with your dog may be solved, but you won't see long-term results if you don't stick to that system and follow through.

The second common issue is that some of the training methods or opinions are outdated and not proven to be effective. Yet professionals use them without considering how to improve or change them before presenting them to the public. Many training systems are overly complicated. When things become complicated, dog owners lose interest. The reality is that many different dog training systems and tools are unnecessary if the right method of training is selected. If people and professionals were educated properly, had learned how to communicate with dogs, and had learned how dogs learn and respond to humans, there would not be the need for certain tools, forceful systems, or even rehabilitation. Humans should be the solution, not the problem.

The third issue is that most people take a training course and don't practice those techniques long enough. They may just practice during the course that they have signed up for and stop right after the course is over. That is not enough for the dog to learn and practice those behaviors. It is not even enough for you to learn and practice whatever you have learned in the course. I get tons of calls from dog owners who have taken an obedience course and they still have some basic issues with their dogs. They think the issue is the trainer or the training system, when in reality it is their lack of consistency and lack of commitment that has resulted in them not being successful and seeing results.

I once met a couple who had adopted a dog that was reactive to other dogs. Every day I would see them walking the dog and working with the dog. They stayed on the plan and the system that they were given by a professional, even though it was not my preferred type of training. At the end, they saw results. The dog was getting less and less reactive to other dogs, to the point that after a few months the dog did not care about other dogs anymore. I was so excited and impressed by the dog owners' commitment that I had to express my feelings to them.

That is why I always feel that humans should be the solution, not the problem. In this case, the humans were the solution.

Creating Balance

You may have heard that dogs should be dominated or that you need to make your dog a follower. The reality is that dogs love to be led and told what to do. It is a natural, genetic behavior. Most dogs love to be told what to do because it makes their lives easier. If a dog has to be in control or in dominant mode, it is like having a long to-do list. The dog is under lots of pressure to fulfill his responsibilities, which results in a lot of stress and anxiety. Less responsibility means less stress, and dogs love that.

There are many pros and cons to dogs in following mode. Let's talk about the pros first, and I will give you an example.

I had a client who loved his job, which was to fix things. He was told what to do and he did it, and he was very happy at the end of each day. He had a dog that he could not control, and it was misbehaving. I asked him about his work and whether he'd liked to advance his career. He told me that he was happy where he was and loved to be told what to do. He did not want to be the boss, because he had seen how stressed out his boss was.

This dog owner did not like to lead. He was happy doing what he was told to do. On the other hand, his dog was not happy because he had to take the boss's position in his family since the owner was not taking that position. This made the dog stressed. In this case, the dog wanted and was asking for the owner to lead. The owner wanted the dog just to do whatever he wanted and act like a normal dog, but he couldn't because the dog loved to be led too. The owner and the dog were both put in positions that were not comfortable or healthy. So they were not a good match because of the positions that they wanted to be in. The owner of the dog couldn't have a well-behaved and balanced dog; he would have had the same issue with any dog due to his lack of leadership ability.

Now imagine the same person doing something he didn't like to do. Let's say that person was forced to boss people around. How would he perform his job? Not as well as when he had been told what to do. Although leadership positions often pay better, they also come with more responsibilities. After a while, this person would stop enjoying going to work, which could cause him to become depressed. There'd be no more joy in life simply because that person was forced to lead when he did not want to.

When a dog is not being led, the dog easily becomes stressed, both physically and mentally, and everything becomes negative. The dog can't relax even though he wants to. When dog owners do not do what they are supposed to do, which is to lead, the dogs have to take that position, which is a job they do not enjoy.

Dogs don't want to make decisions. It is too much work for them. Tell your dog what to do. Show him how to do it. He won't mind and will not hate you for that. He will actually love you instead.

That is the pros of dogs wanting to be led. Just imagine the dog wants to be told what to do. It doesn't get better than that.

All you have to do is just tell and show the dog the way and it will follow.

One of the cons of dogs needing to be told what to do is that you need to be the boss. That means telling your dog what to do at all times. You can't just leave him alone and hope he will learn everything automatically or that he will grow out of undesirable behaviors. You need to take the time to tell him what to do, how to do it and where he is allowed to do it. Training gives you the tools to communicate these expectations to your dog.

Dogs love to have a duty, a job. They simply need to know what they are supposed to do. Do they sleep? Do they sit? Do they walk? Do they need to guard the property? Do they attack? Should they chase the birds or the squirrels? Are they allowed on the couch or not? Once they know, for instance, that they are not allowed on the couch, they will not argue about it. It will allow them not to worry about being on the couch anymore. That's all they want to know, whether they are allowed on the couch or not.

Yes, sleeping becomes a job for them. They need to have clarity about what they are supposed to do. They need to know their roles in relationships and in life. This creates relaxation and peace of mind, which allow them to be balanced.

Dogs are simple creatures, which is why I love living and working with them. They are not as complicated as humans, and it is humans who set them off to develop complications and become complex individuals.

To stop this from happening, you need to know and understand what it is that dogs need to live a healthy, balanced life. By knowing what they need, you have some tools and ideas to work with your dog, rather than against him.

Before getting a dog, you need to discuss the subject with all family members. You will be adding another member to your family, and this needs to be made clear to all current family members. In determining whether to get a dog, or what kind of dog to get, ask the following questions:

- Is it realistic to own a dog?
- Can I/we provide for all the dog's needs?
- Do I/we have the time for an extra family member?
- Do I/we know how to take care of a dog?
- Do I/we know what to feed a dog?
- Can I/we afford the normal and unexpected expenses of having a dog?
- Can I/we provide care to the dog for the next ten to fifteen years?

By having the right answers and a realistic point of view, you can determine if you are ready to have a dog. When you are ready, you will be able to create balance for your dog and yourself by making sure you meet the a dog's five essential needs successfully.

Chapter 2

FIVE: THE MAGIC NUMBER!

Dogs are very intelligent beings—just like humans—and can learn quickly, but too often, dog owners underestimate their dogs' learning ability and end up not approaching this matter appropriately.

The number five has a great meaning in everything that I do, especially when I am trying to learn or teach something. It is a perfect number for repetition when you are trying to memorize, learn, or try something new. Other numbers are either too little or too big. Less than five is not enough to learn sometimes and more than five just becomes repetitive and unnecessary.

I use five repetitions to teach both the owner and the dog a new behavior—sometimes it doesn't even take that long. Each session should include five repetitions of each exercise, especially with puppies and not more than that because puppies get bored easily. I know for sure that a dog can learn a behavior when is repeated five times. Some dogs even learn in less than five repetitions and some need exactly five.

Five is also the number of needs a dog has to have met on a daily basis—and compared to a human, this is very little. These five common dog needs are true for every breed and every size, and they need to be satisfied on a daily basis. Yes, a daily basis. These needs are psychological, physical, social, emotional, and mental needs. If a dog's needs are not satisfied on a daily basis, it can cause the dog to become an unbalanced, unhealthy member of the family, lacking in the knowledge of the meaning of companionship, the concept of cooperativeness, and the ideas essential to love, intimacy, and relationship building.

Most dogs that I work with don't trust humans, even their own family humans. They don't know that they need to cooperate with the humans, and instead they work against them. They have forgotten to love and be loved. They have not learned how to build relationships or even how to learn.

Take a good hard look at your life; if you think you can't meet these five common dog needs on a daily basis, then it is better to avoid getting a dog—at least until the time is right and you are ready to do so.

Fulfilling the five essential dogs' needs could help alleviate the confusion and set some structure and rules for you and your dog to follow.

So let's get started! A dog's five essential needs, which I will discuss in the following chapters, are exercise, training, socialization, care, and affection. Remember, dogs need these on a daily basis and preferably in that order.

Chapter 3

NEED NUMBER ONE: EXERCISE

The first thing a dog needs prior to anything else and at the start of each day is exercise. Let's take a look at the physical benefits of exercise for your dog.

Exercise helps use up oxygen; it causes your dog's body to burn stored fat and helps him maintain a normal weight and a healthy body. Regular, moderate exercise, particularly walking, keeps his bones strong. A physically active dog is much healthier than an inactive one. Exercise also allows the dog to release charged-up energy that has built up overnight or during naps.

Humans need a regular form of exercise, just as dogs do. Regular exercise will keep you healthy, and you will be more productive. Even better is to exercise with your dog. You can go for walks with your dog daily and include your dog in your training or workout sessions.

A new study has shown that most people spend 90 percent of their lives indoors, which is not healthy or natural. A health report published by Harvard Medical School suggests many physical and mental health benefits can be met just by being outdoors. These benefits include your vitamin D level rising, a happier mood, improved concentration, and perhaps even faster healing. So going for a walk with your dog not only is good for your dog, but it is also great for you.

General Benefits of Regular Exercise for Your Dog

- Maintenance of healthy weight
- Reduced stress levels
- Relieved symptoms of depression and anxiety
- Increased healthy energy
- Improved digestion
- Stronger muscles and bones
- Strengthened immune system
- Better quality of life
- More confidence

A regular exercise routine is the ideal for a dog. This means the dog receives the same level and amount of activity on a daily basis, rather than exercising every few days vigorously or having an irregular exercise routine, for example, just on weekends.

You need to provide a simple exercise routine for your dog that is realistic and manageable on a daily basis. You and your dog need to be physically able to perform the exercise routine on a daily basis. A nonassertive, relaxed, and fun form of regular activity or exercise is more ideal than approaching each day with a "Let's do whatever we can today, and we'll see what happens tomorrow."

If your dog gets regular daily exercise, he will be able to tolerate unplanned exercise that may happen here and there, but if you exercise or overexercise your dog on an irregular basis, you are more likely to cause physical injuries.

The idea here is to create balance; by providing regular exercise, you will be able to create balance for your dog.

Who wants a dog that is unable to participate in your daily activities because it is extremely tired? It is more fun to have a dog that is physically and mentally able to join you either on the couch or on a shopping trip to the hardware store.

Many times dog owners view exercise as an outlet for releasing stress in hyper, high-energy dogs. The reality is that exercise should be considered a way of recuperating or relaxing rather than as an outlet to release negative energy.

And this isn't limited to physical exercise. Exercise should be considered twofold—physical and mental. The amount of each that your dog needs will depend on the dog's energy level and personality.

Physical Exercise

It is often easy to only focus on the physical aspect of the exercise—tire out the dog to the point that he can't walk so he stays calm for the rest of the day. This form of exercise is very unhealthy, however, and can lead to mental instability and physical injuries.

Many owners think a tired dog is a well-behaved dog. Not necessarily. It all depends on the dog and the situation. In my opinion, exercising a dog is different from tiring out a dog.

Some dog owners feel the need to tire out their dog in order to get the dog to behave properly. In most cases that is how it appears. Many of my clients say that they see a big difference between when their dog has exercised and when it has not.

This is because ever since their relationship started, the dog owners have unwittingly trained their dogs in a different philosophy: "I will drain you physically so you will not be able to do anything after."

In this philosophy, the body gets tired but the mind has not learned anything, which is the main reason dogs misbehave in the first place.

Let's say a dog is misbehaving by pulling on the leash, barking at strangers and other dogs, jumping on people, and not coming when called. So, one idea is to burn off its energy to tire it out to gain control over the behavior.

The problem is that bad behavior is still there no matter how long you exercise your dog. You need to work on eliminating the bad behavior rather than tiring the dog out. If you focus on tiring out the dog rather than on giving him healthy exercise, you are building a stronger, fitter bad-behaving dog. It is more likely that you will be masking the problem by sweeping it under the rug.

Of course, if you get your dog tired, he won't have the energy to show certain behavior but that may be for only a short period of time, but all the bad behaviors are still there even after exercising the dog for hours. I have seen dogs that can be exercised for many hours and still have the energy to do more activities. These are known as high-energy, hyper dogs that have not learned to slow down.

When exercise is focused on the physical only, we are forcing the body of the dog to do more than it can handle. Dogs genetically and naturally are not designed to be physically active for long periods of time. Their bodies are designed to have short bursts of activity—a five-minute run, a thirty-minute walk, fifteen minutes of play, etc.

Animals, especially hunters or predators, are designed to chase their prey for short bursts or distances, and if they are not successful in catching the prey within that short time, they give up for the day. They conserve their energy, rather than waste it, in case they need to run away to survive.

Dogs know their own physical limitations, but when owners push their limitations by forcing them to run or jog with them or run alongside a bike, it limits the dog's ability to stop and take a break voluntarily.

Dogs don't live for a long time as we do. In the short time they are with us, we cannot force them or allow them to abuse their bodies. Don't assume that the dog can do the same types of exercise that you do all the time. Their life spans are shorter.

Instead, teach them to slow down. If a dog does not learn, he will become a hyper dog. A hyper dog is one that will have a hard time relaxing. He is alert all day long, and if a dog stays in that state of mind, he stays in a mode that I call "the stalking mode."

Some dog owners keep their dogs in stalking mode physically and mentally all day long without even knowing it. Their dogs never get to conserve their energy. Dogs and predators conserve their energy naturally and instinctively and are taught to relax by their parents. In these cases, dogs should be taught by humans to relax, but in human society a dog does not enter a relaxed state of mind regularly.

Most dogs that have been overexercised are stressed, and therefore unbalanced, dogs. Their owners have pushed them to do more than they are capable of. Sometimes this is unintentional; the owners feel that their dogs are high energy and in need of more exercise. Just remember that your dog may be stressed because he is overexercised, not under. If you overexercise a dog that is full of stress and anxiety, you are just going to add more stress and anxiety. An overexercised dog is unable to fully take advantage of the other benefit of exercise—the ability to also relax—and this will always result in a physically fit yet unbalanced dog.

A hyper dog has not learned or experienced calmness and relaxation. A hyper dog needs to learn to relax, to calm down, and he has to experience relaxation many times over a long period of time in order to learn it. This will change his energy levels to normal, and only in this normal state can exercise focus on the mental benefits.

Overexercising a dog causes a few issues such being hyper, excited, and nervous, which lead to an insecure dog that can't relax. It may also lead to the development of physical and mental issues in the future.

The results of extreme exercise with your dog today may result in physical injury tomorrow. Most major injuries or health issues result from minor injuries that have occurred when the dog was younger and the dog was overexercised.

Here are the general negative effects of overexercising dogs:

- Hyperactivity
- Overexcitement
- Physical injuries
- Mental issues
- Inability to relax
- Nervousness
- Insecurity

Frequently, stressed dogs have stressed owners. One reason a dog misbehaves or is unstable is because the dog is stressed because the owners are anxious, emotional, or stressed. Most dog owners have a hard time relaxing in general, especially when their dog is misbehaving or is unstable. Because dog owners haven't taught their dog how to relax, when the dog misbehaves, the owner is not able to calm the dog down.

In order for the dog to relax, the dog owner needs to be relaxed. But relaxation needs to be practiced continuously and consistently before the dog will understand and respond.

Mental Exercise

The mental aspect of exercise is psychological and spiritual stimulation. Most dogs need to have more of this kind of exercise. Dogs need about 70 percent mental stimulation and about 30 percent physical stimulation daily. Therefore, focus on mental stimulation rather than physical stimulation.

A simple sit-and-stay exercise at a traffic intersection is an ideal mental activity. For the dogs who love to sniff, that practice is a very healthy form of mental exercise. It allows the dog to use his natural instincts and do what he loves to do. Sniffing helps his mind take in lots of information. As you may remember, whenever you are in a classroom where you need to take in information, you feel more tired than usual, but in a healthy way.

Mental activities and exercises are much healthier than physical activities.

Lack of exercise is also an epidemic issue with dogs. Most dogs become overweight and unhealthy because they don't get enough exercise or stimulation. Some dogs are left home alone most of the day, getting just a very short walk around the block. These dogs are also stressed and have very limited ways to release their anxiety.

In sum, all dogs need to have a balanced amount of daily physical and mental exercise in order to be healthy and happy.

Ideal Exercise

There are many ways you can exercise your dog. The best way of exercising a dog is combining training with exercise, focusing mainly on mental activity. Walking on- or off- leash (do this only with an off-leash-trained dog) and playing with other dogs are the best forms of exercise.

There are many benefits to walking with your dog, as long as it is done properly and you and your dog are good walking partners. Many dog owners do not know that dogs love leash walks because the owner is in control of the dog. But most dog owners don't like walking their dogs on the leash because the dog does not enjoy walking with the owner. There are a few reasons why dog owners tend to let their dogs off-leash. The dog owners believe that the dog enjoys freedom so they take the dog off-leash or they'll unleash the dog because he can't walk on leash properly.

Walking your dog on a leash allows you and your dog to build a better and healthier relationship. It also allows you to provide your dog with information. Having a dog on-leash gives you the opportunity to manage your dog in such a way that your dog feels you are able to control his responses in any situation and confirm that you are in control. That's what a dog really needs: a human who is in control. This builds a stronger bond and improves the relationship. This is a very important part of having a dog on-leash; it helps you get to know each other better and allows you to work on behaviors your dog needs to improve.

Dog Play

When dogs play, magic happens. Playful dogs love life, are happy, and tend to have fewer behavioral issues, especially if they play and interact with other dogs. They get good physical and mental exercise from it. Allow your dog to play with other dogs every day, if possible.

When a dog plays with other dogs, it helps him learn and practice social skills with other dogs. During play sessions, dogs practice play biting, hunting, killing, and fighting, and they practice caring for other dogs. These are essential skills for dogs to learn, especially when they are young, and dogs should practice play throughout their lives.

A puppy, just like a human newborn, is pure and simple. All it wants to do is eat, sleep, and play. Humans provide the eating (food) and sleeping (shelter) part of dogs' lives very well, but they often don't provide the play (especially with other dogs) part properly, though it is one of the most important parts of a dog's life.

To you and me, the play may look simply fun, but it is more than that. It is the important structural part of building personality, awareness, and characteristics of a dog. It allows your dog to start communicating with other dogs. This communication teaches dogs to learn how to speak dog language and gain social skills. The second part of play is to be invited by other dogs. This allows your dog to be accepted in the animal world. The third part, the physical part of the play, allows the dog to gain survival skills, and the mental part of the play allows your dog to learn problem-solving skills. These skills not only improve the dog's problem-solving in dog interactions but also in interactions with humans and life in general.

Puppies should start playing with other dogs their own size and age in a controlled environment while supervised. At around the age of three to four months, puppies should get involved with larger, older, more mature, well-behaved, social dogs to learn more social skills.

Young dogs need to continue having regular social interactions and playtime with all kinds of dogs in a safe and secure environment with well-balanced, well-behaved dogs who only want to play. For this reason, I suggest daily visits to dog parks, dog day care, or play care in your neighborhood.

There is a time when a young dog will slow down and lose his interest in playing with other dogs. He will be more interested in other activities such as hiking, walking, resting, and maybe spending time with humans. As dogs age, they tend to be less interested in play. The dog physically and mentally is ready to take it easy and relax. This usually happens between the ages of two and five, but until then, you need to keep your dog active playing with other dogs and continue walking them daily. A happy, playful dog will never lack social skills.

Fetch Game

Playing fetch with your dog is another form of healthy activity, as long as it is done in short sessions, such as five- to ten-minute increments, one to two days a week. Longer sessions will cause mental issues and physical injuries. The repetition that fetch requires is too much physical and mental stress when played for a long time. A toy ball is not a good object to be focused on or to socialize with.

However, the game of fetch can be productive and beneficial if it is played properly. It should include some form of training and follow some rules. The main goal is simple, but you and your dog will benefit more if you add some rules. One simple rule to add is that the dog sits and stays; have your dog sit and stay while you throw the ball, and then give the release or fetch command once the ball has been thrown. Another rule you can incorporate is sitting on command or an automatic sit after fetching the ball.

Other Forms of Exercise
Agility
Agility is a dog sport in which a handler directs a dog through an obstacle course in a race for both time and accuracy. Dogs run off-leash with no food or toys as incentives, and the handler can touch neither dog nor obstacles.

Flyball
Flyball is a sport in which teams of dogs race against one another from a start/finish line, over a line of hurdles, to a box that releases a tennis ball whenever a dog presses the spring-loaded pad handler while carrying it.

Rally "O"
Rally obedience (also known as Rally or Rally-O) is a dog sport based on obedience. It was originally devised by Charles L. "Bud" Kramer from the obedience practice of "doodling"—doing a variety of interesting warm-up and freestyle exercises.

Scent Detection
Scent detection is a fun activity with dogs. Any dog can do this. The object is to teach your dog to find an object or specific scent.

Tracking
Tracking is a technique in which dogs are trained to locate certain objects by using the object's scent, for a variety of purposes.

Tracking has always been an essential skill for dogs to survive in the wild, through hunting and tracking down potential prey.

Herding
Herding is a competitive dog sport in which herding dogs move sheep around a field, fences, gates, or enclosures as directed by their handlers.

These are some other forms of activities you can do with your dog, but be careful: Many dog owners either do too much or not enough.

Remember, it is not suitable for a dog to have vigorous exercise only once a week for a couple of hours. It puts a lot of pressure on the dog's joints and muscles. Therefore I recommend practicing these activities more often, at least two days a week and for a few years, so your dog's body, muscles, joints, and mind also get a workout. I also suggest doing these exercises in a noncompetitive form; although the competitive forms are more popular, it doesn't mean it is the right form for you or your dog. In my opinion, competitive training creates negative energy in you, making you feel as if it is OK to push your dog past his limits. Dogs may seem to be having fun, but in fact they just can't help doing what you ask them.

Quantity of Exercise
We can't put an exact number on how much or how long a dog should exercise. It all depends on the age, size, energy level, and physical ability of the dog. Still, as a place to start, the best formula I can suggest is as follows:

- Three months to one year old: four times a day for fifteen minutes each
- One to five years old: two times a day for thirty minutes each
- Five years and older: one time a day for thirty minutes each

You can also add periodic short but healthy amounts of playtime with other dogs during your daily walks so your dog can get his socialization and dog training as well. In the end, don't force your dog to do more than he's capable of. Think about their near future.

Chapter 4

NEED NUMBER TWO: TRAINING

Training a dog has been assigned many meanings and purposes. In my opinion, training is teaching and practicing a new behavior while not practicing and repeating the old or any other unwanted behaviors. It also involves teaching a communication system or a language to a dog so he can understand humans, allowing humans to communicate with him.

Training could involve teaching a dog to stop barking or to stop attacking a person in the same way we teach a dog to sit. Dogs learn by repeating the same exercise or particular behavior over and over until they memorize it. When a dog is reactive to a certain thing, he repeats his reaction every time he encounters it, exercising the behavior over and over again. Therefore, the dog is implementing this reaction as a normal behavior, learning and responding to it. In most cases, the dog needs to cease practicing and repeating the reaction—the unwanted behavior—instead practicing something else—the wanted behavior.

If your dog is chewing your shoes, don't provide an opportunity for your dog to find shoes. If a dog is reacting to something or is responding to a certain behavior, it is because no one has been telling the dog not to practice and to stop that behavior. Many dog owners tell me they try to stop their dogs, but the dog won't stop and sometimes the behavior even gets worse. The issue here is the way that owners try to stop their dogs—yelling at or yanking them, getting angry and emotional, and making some of the common mistakes associated with dogs' bad behavior. Instead, owners need to stay calm and in control so they can help their dogs replace that behavior with something else.

Here are some of the common mistakes dog owners make when training their dog:

- Off-leashing the dog at very young age
- Getting emotional
- Not rewarding the dog for doing something great including even minor accomplishments
- Not correcting the dog for any bad behavior, even minor issues
- Repeating the dog's name over and over as though the dog cannot hear them
- Not being consistent
- Not investing enough time in training

Let's say a dog is reactive to the sound of trucks and starts barking and getting anxious whenever he hears one. If his owner does nothing, the dog will continue to get anxious at the sound of trucks, repeating this behavior until it becomes his normal reaction.

What if, instead of getting angry with the dog, his owner asked him to replace that behavior with something else—perhaps playing with a toy?

Of course, the change won't happen immediately, but dog owners need to start somewhere and continue reinforcing it until the dog learns and repeats playing with the toy instead of reacting negatively to the sound of the truck. The goal in the future should be that as soon as the dog hears truck he will look for the toy. In dog training, this is called association.

Remember that anything you do with your dog is a form of training. Everything that happens throughout each day is a form of training. What we want to implement, however, is called focused training. Focused training involves a dedicated time, a dedicated place, and dedicated energy to training and teaching or practicing certain behaviors.

Focused training can be fifteen or thirty minutes a day for a few months. During this time, you only practice certain things, repeating those and only those things. Let's say you just taught your dog to sit and stay; you need to practice these two commands for fifteen to thirty minutes every day for a few months, repeating, praising, and making the lesson more challenging by expanding the time or changing the training location.

Focus training allows you to input the information rapidly while having fun and allows the dog to learn and practice the behavior faster. When you are done with one specific focused training session, it is time to practice the behavior throughout the day and in real-life scenarios.

The problem that many people face with focused training, however, is that it becomes boring for them, so they don't continue it for a long enough period of time.

Still, focused training is very effective when you need to change an unwanted behavior. Let's use the example of the dog who reacts negatively to the truck. Start by using focused training with the dog away from the truck; create a game with a toy, and play this game with the dog for a while. Then take the dog to a park, and play with the dog and his toy there. Next, take your dog near a truck, and just before the dog reacts to the truck start playing the game learned with focused training. You are replacing the negative reaction (unwanted behavior) with play (wanted behavior). It's that simple!

Dogs want to make their owners happy. They will do anything for owners who have built healthy, real relationships with them—something that is well worth remembering. Many dog owners start training their dogs too early, before they have built relationships with them. It is very common that, when training is not successful, the relationship between dog and owner is not healthy. In this situation, dogs often misbehave—something very common in puppies and newly adopted dogs.

This does not mean, however, that you have to wait to start training with your dog. What it does mean is that you should not expect to see the results you want right away. To see results, you need to spend a lot of quality time with your dog in the beginning of the relationship. You need to get to know each other. Don't rush it; be patient. Spending some time together allows you and your dog to learn about each other and to start building trust. Once trust has been established, then you need to work on building a friendship, which in turn will lead to love.

Starting to train your dog from day one is very important because it helps you to start building the relationship. Your dog does not trust you yet. You know that the dog "belongs" to you, but in your dog's eyes, you don't belong to him yet. The dog needs to learn belonging—and the way a dog learns this is by spending quality time with you. It may take a few weeks, or for some dogs a few months or even years—it depends on the dog, his age, and the way you interact with him.

I have seen dog owners who have had a dog for years, but their dogs still feel and look like they just met their owners a few months ago! I have seen dogs who don't come to their owners when called. The truth is this happens because the dog does not have a healthy relationship with the owner yet—not because the dog has not been trained yet. A dog who loves and respects his owner will go to that person when called without hesitation.

Relationships should be built from both sides. Many issues that face dog owners are because their relationships with their dogs are one-sided. The dog does not see his relationship with the owner as the owner sees it. Materialistic things may make you feel ownership for the dog, but dogs do not see these things in the same light. I have had some dog owners tell me that they rescued a dog years ago, the dog is in a much better place now, but he still reacts to certain things negatively, and they don't understand it. In cases like this, the dog does not trust his owner fully, even after several years. That is a long time for a dog to live like that. Imagine living with a partner for years in fear, without trust, and constantly being anxious. How would you feel?

Unfortunately, the reality is that these dogs have only partially been rescued. However, the good news is that dogs can adapt quickly. They want to live balanced, calm lives when the right situations and conditions have been set.

The first place to start working on behavioral issues with your dog is with an examination of your relationship. A healthy relationship will allow the dog to pay attention to you, listen to you, take clues from you, and be part of your family rather than work against you and deal with situations on his own.

Training in the early stages of the relationship should consist of walking the dog, setting rules, and—most importantly—following them. It is very important to set some rules early on, because they provide you with a guideline to follow. It is much easier to follow a predetermined guideline than to try to come up with something in the moment each time a situation occurs. You also need to make sure you follow the rules. This requires repeating the rules constantly, which translates into consistency. Consistency builds relaxation and trust in your dog. Your dog needs to know what is going to happen next, which will help him relax and calm down.

For example, a rule I have for my dogs is "Dogs shall not get on my couches and beds." This is a personal choice, and it has nothing to do with domination or dictatorship. Now, first, I have to remember this rule at all times. My dog is going to approach the couch and try to get on it. I need to remember the rule and stop my dog from getting on the couch. I can't break the rule just because I've had a bad day at work and I want my dog on my lap, when for the past five days I have been blocking my dog from getting on the couch.

My dog does not know that I had a bad day at work, and therefore I am breaking the rule. My dog does not rationalize why I am changing the rule. From my dog's point of view, I am breaking the rule, period. My dog is going to think, "Well, the human broke the rule as I was just getting to learn this new rule. Am I allowed to break rules?"

The next day, when my dog approaches the couch, I suddenly remember the rule. If I go back to blocking my dog from getting on the couch, my dog is going to be surprised. He will get upset that I am not letting him on the couch. Confusion produces stress, which makes it even harder for him to learn the rule.

Let's say I get up to get a drink, and when I come back, I see my dog on the couch. I ask my dog to get off, but he refuses; I grab his collar to pull him off, and he growls, turns around, and bites my hand. I get hurt and angry, and then I call my dog all sorts of names.

Now, let's analyze this situation. Who is at fault here—me or my dog?

It is very important to set rules and to follow them, both you and your dog. This form of management creates clarity and relaxation. Once the dog knows that rules exist and they need to be followed, your dog will relax and will be able to focus on the rules. You need to make sure that, no matter what, rules are not broken. If you break rules or are not consistent in following them from your dog's point of view, you have fallen back and need to start from zero again.

If you set a rule and have been consistent the past ninety-nine times, and all of a sudden you forget or break the rule on the hundredth time, all of the ninety-nine practices are gone, and you need to start from zero again.

This is because your dog is trying to test and teach you to be consistent. That is why it looks like your dog is not learning when in fact your dog is helping you learn how to be committed and consistent.

I would like to note here that following up on a rule is different from teaching a new rule. First you need to teach your dog a new rule using commands. Teaching a new rule could be, for instance, not allowing the dog on the couch and getting the dog to sit and stay in front of the couch rather than getting on it.

Asking your dog to stop barking at guests is setting a rule, and asking your dog to sit and stay while you greet guests as they enter your house is using a command that helps to implement the rule more easily. This is following up on the rule. Repeating the rule over and over until it becomes a habit. Once you set a rule, you need to teach that rule to the dog somehow, and that is when you use commands. You need to teach the dog to sit and stay on command, for instance.

Before teaching new rules to dogs, first write down the rules for yourself. Divide a page into two sections. On one side write what the dog is allowed to do, and on the other side write what the dog is not allowed to do. Make copies and stick them in several places around your house so everyone can see and be reminded of the rules. This will help keep all family members on the same page.

Now that the rules are set, you just need to implement them. The way you implement the rules is by being consistent and following the rules on every occasion and in every situation for a few months. This is the hard part; one thing that can help get the process going is to take a basic obedience course. You'll be able to learn the rules and basic commands to teach the rules to your dog.

Next, keep in mind the five-times rule. If you are teaching something to your dog and you need to repeat it more than five times, most likely you are doing something wrong. One of the most common reasons for failure is not being consistent, which can cause your dog to be unable to learn quickly. Another reason could be because you have not spent the minimum of fifteen minutes a day needed to focus train your dog. Other reasons include not being familiar enough with the techniques to use them properly or getting too emotional during the training.

Just step back and relax. Find out which part of your approach is not working or is weak. Be realistic and honest. Don't blame the dog. Take responsibility, but don't punish yourself. There is no shame in admitting mistakes. You are not judging your dog or yourself by doing this. Focus on the goal of helping your dog.

Although training your dog will help you solve many issues, redirect behaviors, and teach new behaviors, it has its limitations. One limitation is with extreme behaviors. In extreme forms of developed behaviors such as aggression, you will most likely need to rehabilitate your dog. Rehabilitation is different from training.

Training helps your dog build new desirable behaviors and learn to avoid developing unwanted behaviors. Rehabilitation is working with a dog that has already developed unwanted behaviors; it is a matter of undoing these behaviors in an extreme way. In a nutshell, training is to prevent damage from occurring, while rehabilitation is what is done to fix the damage.

In rehabilitation dog experts use tools and techniques and work one-on-one with the dog on a psychological level throughout the day for weeks or even months. Some of the signs that indicate that a dog may need rehabilitation rather than training are when a dog is extremely aggressive toward other dogs and people. When a dog is extremely fearful of people, other dogs, or anything, it is a danger to society.

But how would an owner go about rehabilitating a dog? The answer is somewhat cold-hearted or cruel. There may be two types of solutions. One may be that the dog has been in your care and he has become a very unbalanced, unstable dog in your care. Obviously you won't be able to rehabilitate the dog. You have caused the dog to get where he is today. You won't have the time and the techniques and the knowledge to rehabilitate. The best option here would be to ask a professional to help you with that, which often means the dog has to be living with the person who will be rehabilitating the dog for a long time or maybe even forever.

The other type is that you may adopt a dog that needs rehabilitation and you feel confident that you are capable of rehabilitating and training the dog. In this case you may be a person who is knowledgeable about dogs, is balanced emotionally and mentally, and has all the time in the world to work on the dog.

One more thing you need to know is that training a dog comes only after it has been rehabilitated. You can't train a dog who is emotionally and mentally unbalanced. You need to create balance in his life with rehabilitation and then teach new rules using training.

Chapter 5

NEED NUMBER THREE: SOCIALIZATION

Socialization in many ways is a form of prevention of dogs developing antisocial behaviors. There are many kinds of antisocial behaviors.

Antisocial behaviors can be different from one family to another, but there are certain behaviors that tend to be standard for social or antisocial behaviors in our human and urban lifestyle. Some people let their dogs on the couch as a very normal occurrence, considering it a social behavior. Others consider it a very bad behavior, therefore making it an antisocial behavior.

Here is a list of some social behaviors that are generally considered necessities for dogs today:

- Greeting other dogs and people properly
- Staying calm when guests arrive
- Staying calm while watching people and dogs pass by the window
- Ignoring birds and cats
- Playing with other dogs
- Obeying humans
- Not peeing and marking inside the house

Socialization of a dog should not be limited to humans or other dogs only. Dogs need to be exposed to many things from a young age, such as cars, streets, buses, trees, garbage cans, boxes, chairs, and cats.

Here is a list of antisocial behaviors that are generally considered unacceptable for dogs today:

- Jumping on people and other dogs
- Growling at people
- Attacking people and other dogs
- Jumping and barking when guests arrive
- Barking at everything that passes by the window
- Chasing, attacking, and barking at cats and birds
- Ignoring and disrespecting humans
- Marking at every opportunity, both inside and outside

Of course, there are other behaviors that could be considered social or antisocial, but most of these are subjective according to each individual and family.

Socialization is to some degree natural behavior for domesticated dogs. All breeds are bred to be social with humans, other dogs, and animals. Unfortunately, some dogs have lost their social skills, often because they did not get proper or enough socialization on a regular basis, especially when they were young.

When you force a social animal like a dog to be limited in its social activities, he has no choice but to become unbalanced and act unusual. Most bad behaviors are developed because dogs are not given the opportunity to play and socialize with other dogs, especially when they are young and their brains are hungry for knowledge. This is when they need to learn proper behavior rather than unusual behaviors.

Socialization should start from no later than four weeks of age and continue vigorously until two years of age. After two years, dogs still need to socialize to maintain their social skills, and socialization should continue throughout their lives.

A dog should learn and maintain social skills from his human. Dogs are expected to live in an unnatural environment for them and in conditions that are strange to them. There are buildings, streets, buses, fireworks, kids, unstable humans, etc., that can startle a young dog.

These are not usually normal things for dogs to live with, but they can be conditioned to tolerate them. The process of teaching dogs to tolerate things can be considered socialization. Usually a dog's canine parents would take care of this, but since humans have taken charge of the dog, they need to teach the dog how to be social.

The socialization of a dog should not be limited to exposing him to humans or other dogs. Dogs need to be exposed to many things from a young age—cars, streets, buses, trees, garbage cans, vacuum cleaners, boxes, chairs, and cats, just to name a few.

Although these seem like obvious things, many dogs are not exposed enough to them because dog owners don't realize they are issues they need to be concerned with. You may think that dogs should automatically be OK with, let's say, a vacuum cleaner, but they are not. They need to be introduced to one and then exposed to it as often as possible without any negative experiences. The introduction must be by you, someone they trust, and must happen for a period of time until they feel comfortable around the vacuum cleaner. Otherwise the vacuum cleaner will become a shock, and the dog will react to it. Once the dog reacts to something, it is the start of the development of unwanted behavior. This is how most unwanted behaviors and antisocial behaviors in dogs are developed. By repetition, they develop and then nurture the behavior.

In many cases a dog may react to a strange item or situation and overcome it with no problems, but sometimes it is the way you follow through the situation that initiates a negative effect. Let's say you have just let the dog investigate the vacuum cleaner, and the dog has come up with a decision about it, but then you step in. The dog investigated and got over it, but right at the time that the dog was walking away, you start petting him vigorously and say, "It's OK, baby, it's just a vacuum cleaner, good boy. It's not going to hurt you."

This simple gesture will actually confirm for the dog that there was actually something wrong with the situation, and he should be more cautious about the vacuum cleaner next time.

In most cases dogs can figure things out and deal with them easily, but they need you to guide them just by introducing the situation or the object. You need to react in a neutral way when the dog reacts in an extreme way. They just need your assurance that they are doing the right thing.

The idea of socializing is not only to make dogs more relaxed around unfamiliar objects. It is also to build confidence and trust between you and your dog. Once there is trust between you and your dog, everything else starts to improve. The trust creates relaxation in the dog when he focuses on you and your directions, allowing him to gain information with a calm state of mind and in a positive form. This state of mind helps the dog gain confidence. A dog that has confidence tends to approach situations positively and without any negative feelings while making accurate decisions, leading to a better chance of living a more relaxed, less anxious, more healthy life.

One of the ways you can help your dog have a proper socialization experience is by using obedience techniques to control the dog physically and therefore mentally, so you can input appropriate information into the dog.

Basic obedience training is the key and the beginning of building a connection with your dog. It will allow you to learn techniques that will help you have verbal and physical communication with your dog. If you learn, for instance, how to get your dog to sit and stay, when you meet a friend or someone on your walk, you can ask your dog to sit and stay so your friend can greet your dog. Your dog can learn how best to greet your friend or even other dogs, rather than jumping on them.

If your dog approaches humans and other dogs in an improper way, it may translate to other dogs in different ways. This may result in a negative outcome and may also look as though your dog is invading their space, which shows that your dog is lacking social skills. Your dog may get attacked by other dogs, and you will blame the other dogs. In reality, you may be approaching a dog who is expecting you and your dog to behave respectfully and have social skills.

I believe if you control your dog and teach your dog to behave well, you will automatically control other dogs, their owners, and the environment. That itself will be a great way of socializing your dog.

Chapter 6

NEED NUMBER FOUR: CARE

Most dog owners provide very good care for their dogs—almost too good. What most of them don't know is that there's a difference between taking care of their dogs and spoiling them. Take care of them with material things and the best food you can afford, but don't spoil them mentally. Most dogs in North America live better lives, materially, than some kids in other countries do.

However, what I want to focus on here about the care that dogs need is the physical care. Everything you have done so far has been to provide mental care for your dog. Now it's time to provide some physical care. You need to physically check your dog on a daily basis from his head to his tail. The following are just a few things that need to be checked and addressed on a daily basis.

Visual Check
The most basic thing you need to do is a visual check of your dog from his head to his tail. This can be done while you are sitting and watching your favorite TV show. Check to see if there are any abnormalities in any part of your dog's body. If you do this daily, you will get to know your dog's body shape, and you will be able

to recognize any lump, bump or scratch that was not there the day before.

I recommend doing a visual check of your dog's ears, eyes, mouth, nose , paws, stomach, and tail every day. Some parts of your dog's body need to be taken care of on a daily basis and some just need periodic care. For instance, you need to brush your dog's fur, no matter how short or long, on a daily basis, but your dog's ears need to be cleaned only when they are dirty.

Diet

The other important part of your dog's care is his diet. There are several types of diets on the market these days. The days of feeding dog just kibble (dry food) should be over, even though kibble remains a staple in most dogs' diets.

When feeding your dog, consider the following:

- Are your dog's stools the same amount or more than the amount he is being fed? If more, then the food that your dog is eating contains too many fillers and not enough nutrition. Most of the times dogs have bad, unhealthy, undigested, smelly, runny stool that dog owners feel is normal. It is not normal for a dog to have bulky, unhealthy stools on a regular basis.
- Does your dog's stool contain undigested particles? If so, your dog is having digestion issues, and you should provide better-quality food.
- Is your dog having diarrhea regularly? If so, the chemicals and preservatives in your dog's food are having an effect on your dog's body.
- Is your dog visiting the vet too often—for example, once a month or even a few times a year? If so, you need to feed your dog better-quality food.

- Is your dog drinking lot of water? If so, that could be a sign of dehydration, which is most likely the result of feeding your dog dry food or kibble. Change your dog's food.

Providing good food will not only help your dog live a healthier life but will also help him thrive in it. Look for dog food other than kibbles. Explore and educate yourself about the new kinds of dog food.

You need to understand and accept that your dog is an animal and a carnivore. An animal's diet is somewhat different from a human diet. Animals cannot be fed human food or even processed food. It simply does not sit well with your dog's digestive system.

Dogs need to eat a balanced, natural, unprocessed diet, which kibble does not provide. A balanced diet for a dog is simple: water; protein in the form of unprocessed natural meat; fresh green vegetables; and supplements like oils, vitamins, and minerals. Most holistic vets will suggest feeding your dog either a raw diet or a home-cooked diet.

By changing your understanding of what you need to feed your dog and the way you provide that food to your dog, you will not only keep him healthier and happier, you can make him balanced mentally and physically.

Your dog relies on you for everything in his life including his diet. He depends on you to provide a diet that he deserves. No one can make that choice and provide for your dog other than you. You have made the choice to bringing him into your life, not the other way around. He has no choice but to comply with your decisions. Your dog needs to eat the food that nature planned for him. He depends on that natural food to survive and live a better life.

The main contributor to your dog's healthy body is the food he takes in. Basically, the saying "you are what you eat" is true in this instance. If you feed your dog a clean, fresh, balanced diet, he will thrive, but if you don't, he will survive yet decay and age faster and have many health issues.

By making some changes in understanding what you need to feed your dog and the way you provide that food to him, you will not only keep him healthier and happier, you can make him balanced mentally and physically.

Domesticated animals' diets are also different from wild animals' diets. Domesticated animals' diets have changed radically throughout the centuries. Today, dogs need to have a different diet system, which kibble does not provide, no matter how much the food companies try to add ingredients to it, simply because the method is wrong and it is not what nature intended.

Traveling in a Car
Your dog must travel in the backseat of a car and must be harnessed in or attached to the seat belt. You can also put him in a kennel or crate in the back of the car.

Grooming
Your dog needs to be groomed on a regular basis. Along with the baths you give him, grooming involves being washed and detailed by a professional who has the skills and equipment necessary to do a more thorough cleaning. I suggest grooming your dog every season, so about four times a year. A trip to the groomer also offers an opportunity to reinforce socialization for your dog.

Nail Clipping
If you don't feel comfortable clipping your dog's nails or don't know how to do it, I suggest taking your dog to a groomer. It is better if your dog is not traumatized when his nails get clipped, which can make it even harder to clip them in the future.

Fur Brushing
Whether your dog has long or short fur, you need to get the right brush and brush him on a daily basis. You can do this while you are watching TV or whenever you are spending quality time with your dog.

Teeth Brushing
Just as humans need to brush their teeth, dogs need their teeth brushed too. Think of it as an act of prevention. Brushing your dog's teeth will prevent lots of toothaches and health issues caused by dental issues including gum disease, pneumonia, kidney disease, heart disease, and cancer. Get used to the physical aspects and the idea of brushing your dog's teeth. You don't need to do it every day (although there is nothing wrong with that), but it should be done at least twice a week.

Vaccination
More and more vets and professionals are agreeing and suggesting not overvaccinating dogs. Overvaccination has resulted in many side effects including health issues and even cancer. Ask your vet to perform a titer blood test annually. The titer test detects the presence and measures the amount of antibodies within a dog's blood. The amount and diversity of antibodies correlates to the strength of the body's immune response.

Spaying or Neutering
The number one reason dogs need to be neutered and spayed is because we don't need more unwanted dogs in shelters. There are many opinions about at what age a dog should be spayed or neutered. I suggest spaying or neutering your puppy at the age of six months. This is the age the dog has physically completed 80 percent of its physical growth and the body is ready to deal with surgeries and healing.

A dog that has not been spayed or neutered smells different from other dogs, and this odor can make him stand out and become a target. After all, most dogs are spayed or neutered. Most dogs will be aggressive toward an unneutered dog because of the active sex hormones, and if that becomes a normal reaction your dog gets from other dogs, it becomes a learned behavior. When a young dog grows up getting those reactions, it becomes a bad situation. You don't want your dog to get used to aggressive behavior.

Other negative side effects of a dog that has not been spayed or neutered is urine marking or excessive urinating and aggression and mounting both in male or female dogs. A dog that thinks and worries about where and when to pee next is an anxious dog.

These days, dogs can get the surgery done in a day and recover within five days. During those five days dogs, need to be immobile and maybe carried around, so I suggest taking a few days off work so you have time to look after your dog. During the recovery, if possible, continue to try to provide for their five daily needs.

These are just a few of the things you need to do to take care of your dog. There are many other areas that you need to look after. Make sure to get used to checking your dog from head to tail daily.

Chapter 7

NEED NUMBER FIVE: AFFECTION

Being affectionate is the most vulnerable part of owning a dog. Humans and dogs experience this state of mind differently. Affection makes humans feel good; we use it to heal emotional wounds, helps us to help others, etc.—which are all very positive, healthy, and effective for humans. Humans need affection at all stages of their lives.

But affection works differently in dogs, and in the animal world at large. This is apparent the most in dogs when they are spoiled emotionally to the point that affection loses its meaning or—even worse—has a negative effect. Don't get me wrong; I am not saying affection is not a good thing to share with a dog, but for dogs, sometimes too much of a good thing can be harmful.

When it comes to affection with dogs, humans make two mistakes. They share affection at the wrong time and place, and they get emotional.

Humans fall into what I call the "love trap." A dog owner falls in love with a dog and soon after adores the dog; the dog becomes the idol that his human carries around, and the human does whatever he "says," offering him whatever he wants. Humans lose all their power to control themselves and become helpless, even if their dogs are creating a nuisance or have become unstable. Dog owners become servants and serve their dogs with no questions.

It is important when you deal with your dog to make sure that you are in a stable state of mind so both you and your dog can relax and teach and learn from each other

In this state, the human becomes a weak individual or source of energy that has lost all power. That is why it is very important, when you start a relationship with a dog, to not fall in love first and to not allow affection to influence the relationship; we all know love is blind. This form of energy is not ideal for building a relationship with a dog.

Dogs and other animals do not share affection the way we do. For them, affection is given only for certain reasons and at certain times of the day. Most animals have a job during the day. They are on watch duty, baby-sitting, scavenging, moving as a group, and most of all surviving. They don't have time to share affection with others constantly. There are certain times of the day that they share affection with a partner and, of course, with puppies.

Humans, on the other hand, share affection with their dogs all day, every day. This is unusual and unnatural for dogs. This causes dogs to develop unbalanced states of mind.

Dogs are constantly showered with love all day without you even knowing it. I call this "ordinary love." You share your space with your dog, you feed him (free) two to three times a day, you walk your dog a few times a day, you brush him, you praise him for doing something right—these are all different forms of affection. Dog owners don't realize this part of their relationship with their dogs is considered affection. On top of all this, dog owners still take the time to have their dogs on their laps and to pet them—although most of the time, this activity is for the dog owners' enjoyment.

If you can remind yourself that you share affection with your dog all day and save the more intimate forms of affections to implement wanted and desired behaviors, then you can create balance and be more effective in creating what you are looking for.

Affection in dogs can be used as a tool to heal, help, and reward. I compare it to a free cookie. It is available to share anytime and it is free, but just because it is free and always available does not mean you or your dog will benefit from it. What happens when you give away free cookies? After a while, they lose their value and the enjoyment they gave in the beginning.

The most common way for humans to approach dogs, whether they have emotional or mental issues, is with emotions (affection). This happens especially when people have just gotten a dog or rescued a dog from a shelter. The problem with establishing a relationship first based on affection is that it will not be a solid one—relationships have to be established on trust and friendship. Remember the free cookie theory? Your dog needs first to trust you, believe in you, and then feel comfortable to receive affection from you. You are going to share "ordinary love" automatically from the moment your dog arrives in your home, anyway. Your dog expects you to respect and work on the relationship rather than explode with emotions, especially affection. When a dog arrives in your home, he is already filled with emotions—fear, stress, anger, confusion, sadness, even excitement. These states of mind are not ideal states in which your dog would benefit from typical affection, and affection may actually work negatively because his mind is so stressed and unbalanced that it can't focus on the benefits of affection.

In other cases—let's say the dog is angry and you share affection with that dog—you will encourage the dog to be furious rather than to calm down. The example I usually see is when a dog is out walking on his leash and is barking at another dog. The dog owners gently pet their dog and say, "It's OK, honey; it's just a dog."

This encourages the dog to be more reactive, because he takes the affection as if he were being rewarded for doing something right—barking at a dog. So, in this situation, the affection has a negative effect.

Also important in all this is your state of mind when you share affection with your dog. Most of the time, when we want to teach a dog something, we approach the lesson as stopping the dog from repeating an action rather than teaching the dog not to do it in the first place. The difference is very important to understand. When you correct or teach something, you are in a neutral state of mind, but when you want to stop a certain behavior, you are emotionally invested—angry, excited, mad, sad, or even scared.

When you deal with a situation emotionally, you are not acting or behaving normally. In a sense, you are not stable yourself; therefore, your dog does not see you as a balanced person. This is why most dog owners do not see results when correcting or taking control of their dogs.

I will give you an example. In my group training classes, I tend to use some of the dogs' behaviors as examples to make visualization and learning easier. Sometimes I use a dog and a dog owner to demonstrate something easy, but I can tell that the dog owner is nervous—maybe because of the pressure of being singled out. Simply asking his or her dog to sit becomes the most difficult task, just because the dog owner becomes nervous and the dog feels that and wants to get away. The dog owner thinks the dog is the worst dog in the class, but as soon as I explain the situation, everybody's lightbulb goes on. That is one of the reasons why I love working with dog owners.

It is important when you deal with your dog to make sure you are in a stable state of mind, so both you and your dog can relax and teach and learn from each other.

Humans naturally try to solve their issues with their dogs through affection. Showing affection is not the same thing as understanding how animals live and form their relationships with their humans. Loving something does not make it perfect, especially when it comes to dogs.

Relax, calm down, and practice relaxation all the time, especially when you are around your dog. If you don't see results or changes in your dog, it may be that your dog is still teaching you to relax completely. Until then, just try to work on it.

Chapter 8

FINAL THOUGHTS

Having a perfect, balanced dog is the goal of every dog owner. I know for sure that there isn't and won't ever be a perfect dog as long as there is no perfect human. As a human being who chooses to get a dog, it is your duty to provide the best for your dog in all ways.

Life with dogs shouldn't be hard—and it isn't, as long as you know what their needs are and you are able to meet those needs.

Although we need to teach dogs many things in order for them to live healthy, balanced lives with us, we also need to learn from them. They teach us many things that we never thought were necessary for us to learn.

Dogs can be our teachers if we take the time to learn from them and accept change. Life without a dog is a life without connection to the reality of life and without a connection to nature.

The question most people ask themselves when getting a dog is, "What do I want from my dog?" The answer is often one of the following: "A dog who can satisfy my needs." "A dog who can be my companion." "A dog I can cuddle with." "A dog I can hike or jog with." "A dog who can play with me and my children." Although these are lofty ideas for acquiring a dog, owning one involves a far different mind-set.

The reality is many people live lives that don't always have room for a dog. From busy work schedules, children's sports, and Internet-driven downtime, this stressful and hyperactive lifestyle often leaves your dog without enough attention and socialization. Some dogs can adapt, *but* the consequences are seldom good.

Naturally, to own a dog you must first be a dog lover. But more important, you need to be an animal lover. And to love animals you must understand them and respect their habits, which are a far cry from ours. Many of us regard dogs as pets, but they are still part animal—perhaps not as wild as wolves, but clearly not as sophisticated as people. So it's important that you understand your dog is an animal first and then a pet.

People need to realize the facts before getting a dog. Either a puppy or a rescued dog comes with tremendous responsibilities that many people are not mindful of. Most are not intentionally acting in this manner, but it has become a casual act of window-shopping: "Isn't it cute! I'd like one!" Dogs should not be considered a product. Seriously ask yourself, "Am I prepared to care for and nurture this animal for the next twelve to sixteen years?"

You are the one who ultimately decides to bring a dog into your life, not the other way around. You need to plan and understand what is involved with owning a dog before moving ahead. The cute puppy stage doesn't last. Puppies grow up, need training, eat more, and demand more. And when dogs grow old, they require special care. Can you commit to this?

Stop asking yourself, "What do I want from a dog?" But ask yourself, "What does a dog need?" Not many people ask this question when they get a dog.

Some people assume dogs need only food, water, shelter, and love. They believe that as long as they can provide these for their dog, it will be happy. Yes, these are essentials for a dog, but not needs. Needs are based on factors designed in their genes and are requirements for a healthy, natural life. Just as people differ, dogs' needs differ as well in temperament and activity and care.

Learn from your dog to become a better person; this only happens when you choose to be open to change and be one with your animal. Feel lucky that you are able to live with a dog.

ABOUT THE AUTHOR

Saro is a certified expert dog trainer who has been working with dogs for more than ten years.

Saro's passion for training dogs and educating dog owners started soon after he opened his "playcare" in 2006. He is committed to being the best dog trainer, training dogs without treats, food, tools, fear, or submission. Rather than using treats or gimmicks such as shock collars, Saro's training methods help dog owners understand how to use their dogs' natural intelligence to achieve success.

Saro, his wife, and their two beagles live and work in beautiful North Vancouver, British Columbia, Canada, where he has been operating Jonah's Ark Doggie Playcare & Training for the past eight years.

Made in the USA
Charleston, SC
10 April 2015